CALL ME ISHMAEL TONIGHT

Agha Shahid Ali

W. W. NORTON & COMPANY   NEW YORK   LONDON

Call Me Ishmael Tonight

A BOOK OF GHAZALS

For information about permission to reproduce selections from
this book, write to Permissions, W. W. Norton & Company Inc.,
500 Fifth Avenue, New York, NY 10110

Manufacturing by The Courier Companies, Inc.
Book design by Chris Welch
Production manager: Andrew Marasia

Library of Congress Cataloging-in-Publication-Data
Agha, Shahid Ali, date.
   Call me Ishmael tonight: a book of ghazals / Agha Shahid Ali. — 1st ed.
      p. cm.
ISBN 0-393-05195-1
1. Ghazals, American. I. Title.
PR9499.3.A39 C35 2003
821'.914 — dc21   2002015950

W. W. Norton & Company Inc., 500 Fifth Avenue, New York, NY 10110
www.wwnorton.com

W. W. Norton & Company Ltd., Castle House, 75/76 Wells Street, London W1T 3Q

1 2 3 4 5 6 7 8 9 0

for Christopher Merrill

Contents

I Have Loved   23

Arabic   24

For You   26

By Exiles   28

Of It All   30

In Real Time   32

Of Fire   34

Things   36

Shines   38

My Word   40

From The Start   42

Angels   44

Of Water   46

As Ever   48

Land   50

Not All, Only A Few Return   52

Even The Rain   53

Water   55

Of Snow   57

Air   59

About Me   60

In Marble   62

Bones   64

In   66

Beyond English   68

Of Light   70

Stars   72

For Time   73

God   75

Forever   77

After You   79

In Arabic   80

Tonight   82

Existed   84

Acknowledgments

Ghazals traditionally do not have titles, and most of these, in earlier or later versions, appeared simply under "Ghazal." For convenience, I have now titled most of them after their refrains.

Acumen: "Of Water"
The Annual of Urdu Studies: "Angels," "By Exiles," "In," "Of It All,"
   "Of Water"
Antioch Review: "In Marble"
Boston Review: "In Real Time"
Chicago Review: "Angels"
Grand Street: "Arabic"

Interim: "About Me"

Massachusetts Review: "Tonight"

Many Mountains Moving: "Of Fire"

The Nation: "Not All, Only A Few Return," "Forever"

The New Republic: "My Word"

The New Yorker: "Beyond English," "Of Snow"

The Paris Review: "For You"

Partisan Review: "From the Start"

Persimmon: "In Real Time"

Poetry: "Land," "Of Light"

Poetry Pilot: "From The Start"

Quarterly West: "Of Water"

Slate: "For Time"

Salt Hill Journal: "In Arabic"

TriQuarterly: "By Exiles," "Of It All"

Verse: "Bones," "God"

Washington Post BookWorld: "In Arabic"

Western Humanities Review: "Shines"

Yale Review: "Even The Rain"

Some of these ghazals also appeared in the following anthologies:

The New Bread Loaf Anthology of Contemporary American Poetry
  ("In Arabic," "Of Water"), *The Norton Anthology of Love*
  ("From The Start"),

and in two previous collections of the author:

The Beloved Witness: Selected Poems ("Arabic") and *The Country Without
  a Post Office* ("Arabic," "Tonight").

Foreword

. . . do as thou art bidden;
thou shalt find me, God willing,
one of the steadfast

—THE KORAN
SURAH 37:102

IN THE SIGNATURE couplet of "Arabic," one of the ghazals in this volume, the poet says, "They ask me to tell them what Shahid means— / Listen: it means 'The Beloved' in Persian, 'witness' in Arabic." Agha Shahid Ali, "the beloved witness," witnesses the world here from an even more unique vantage point than in his previous volumes. During the time when he wrote most of these ghazals, Shahid was confronting his own mortality while undergoing treatment for brain cancer. In some of the ghazals, using a line or a phrase from an American poet, he salutes the craft of those whom he knew and loved. In other searingly honest ghazals he courageously faces death.

Shahid worked assiduously to establish a place in American literature for the formal discipline of the ghazal. He often used the phrase "the ghazal in America" in conversation, and invited American poets to contribute to the anthology he edited, *Ravishing DisUnities: Real Ghazals in English*. Now, in this posthumous volume, Shahid offers us his own American ghazals. The couplets, "gems that can be plucked" from the ghazal's necklace, shine with Shahid's brilliance. Again, he is educating the reader: Making clear that while a ghazal's couplets do not require a narrative continuity, they do have an emotional coherence.

The story of Ishmael in the Holy Koran made an indelible impression on Shahid. Directed by God, Abraham says to his son, Ishmael, "I see in a vision that I offer thee in sacrifice." Differing from the Old Testament story of Abraham and Isaac, the sacrifice is demanded not only of Abraham, but also of Ishmael. Ishmael's willingness to be sacrificed (as in the above epigraph) heightens the beauty of God's redemption where He says: "This is indeed a manifest trial."

Shahid died on December 8, 2001.

—Agha Iqbal Ali and Hena Zafar Ahmad

The Ghazal

THE GHAZAL CAN be traced back to seventh-century Arabia. In its canonical Persian (Farsi) form, arrived at in the eleventh century, it is composed of autonomous or semi-autonomous couplets that are united by a strict scheme of rhyme, refrain, and line length. The opening couplet sets up the scheme by having it in both lines, and then the scheme occurs only in the second line of every succeeding couplet— i.e., the first line (same length) of every succeeding couplet sets up a suspense, and the second line (same length but with the rhyme and refrain—the rhyme immediately preceding the refrain) delivers on that suspense by amplifying, dramatizing, imploding, exploding.

—*Agha Shahid Ali*

CALL ME ISHMAEL TONIGHT

I Have Loved

I must go back briefly to a place I have loved
to tell you those you will efface I have loved.

Arabic

The only language of loss left in the world is Arabic—
These words were said to me in a language not Arabic.

Ancestors, you've left me a plot in the family graveyard—
Why must I look, in your eyes, for prayers in Arabic?

Majnoon, his clothes ripped, still weeps for Laila.
O, this is the madness of the desert, his crazy Arabic.

Who listens to Ishmael? Even now he cries out:
Abraham, throw away your knives, recite a psalm in Arabic.

From exile Mahmoud Darwish writes to the world:
You'll all pass between the fleeting words of Arabic.

The sky is stunned, it's become a ceiling of stone.
I tell you it must weep. So kneel, pray for rain in Arabic.

At an exhibition of Mughal miniatures, such delicate calligraphy:
Kashmiri paisleys tied into the golden hair of Arabic.

The Koran prophesied a fire of men and stones.
Well, it's all now come true, as it was said in the Arabic.

When Lorca died, they left the balcony open and saw:
his *qasidas* braided, on the horizon, into knots of Arabic.

Memory is no longer confused, it has a homeland—
Says Shammas: Territorialize each confusion in a graceful Arabic.

Where there were homes in Deir Yassein, you'll see dense forests—
That village was razed. There's no sign of Arabic.

I too, O Amichai, saw the dresses of beautiful women.
And everything else, just like you, in Death, Hebrew, and Arabic.

They ask me to tell them what Shahid means—
Listen: it means "The Beloved" in Persian, "witness" in Arabic.

For You

Did we run out of things or just a name for you?
Above us the sun doubles its acclaim for you.

Negative sun or negative shade pulled from the ground . . .
and the image brought in one ornate frame for you.

At my every word they cry, "Who the hell are you?"
What would you reply if they thus sent Fame to you?

What a noise the sentences make writing themselves—
Here's every word that we used as a flame for you.

I remember your wine in my springtime of sorrow.
Now the world lies broken. Is it the same for you?

Because in this dialect the eyes are crossed or quartz,
A STATUE A RAZOR A FACT I exclaim for you.

The birthplace of written language is bombed to nothing.
How neat, dear America, is this game for you?

The angel of history wears all expressions at once.
What will you do? Look, his wings are aflame for you.

On a visitor's card words are arranged in a row—
Who was I? Who am I? I've brought my claim. For you.

A pity I don't know if you're guilty of something!
I would—without your knowing—take the blame for you.

Still for many days the rain will continue to fall . . .
A voice will say, "I'm burning, God, in shame for You."

Something like smoke rises from the snuffed-out distance . . .
Whose house did that fire find which once came for you?

God's dropped the scales. Whose wings will cover me, Michael?
Don't pronounce the sentence Shahid overcame for you.

(FOR MICHAEL PALMER)

By Exiles

Where should we go after the last frontiers,
where should the birds fly after the last sky?
—MAHMOUD DARWISH

In Jerusalem a dead phone's dialed by exiles.
You learn your strange fate: you were exiled by exiles.

You open the heart to list unborn galaxies.
Don't shut that folder when Earth is filed by exiles.

Before Night passes over the wheat of Egypt,
let stones be leavened, the bread torn wild by exiles.

Crucified Mansoor was alone with the Alone:
God's loneliness—just His—compiled by exiles.

By the Hudson lies Kashmir, brought from Palestine—
It shawls the piano, Bach beguiled by exiles.

Tell me who's tonight the Physician of Sick Pearls?
Only you as you sit, Desert child, by exiles.

Match Majnoon (he kneels to pray on a wine-stained rug)
or prayer will be nothing, distempered mild by exiles.

"Even things that are true can be proved." Even they?
Swear not by Art but, dear Oscar Wilde, by exiles.

Don't weep, we'll drown out the Calls to Prayer, O Saqi—
I'll raise my glass before wine is defiled by exiles.

Was—after the last sky—this the fashion of fire:
autumn's mist pressed to ashes styled by exiles?

If my enemy's alone and his arms are empty,
give him my heart silk-wrapped like a child by exiles.

Will you, Beloved Stranger, ever witness Shahid—
two destinies at last reconciled by exiles?

(FOR EDWARD W. SAID)

Of It All

I say *This, after all, is the trick of it all*
when suddenly you say, "Arabic of it all."

After Algebra there was Geometry—and then Calculus—
But I'd already failed the arithmetic of it all.

White men across the U.S. love their wives' curries—
I say *O No!* to the turmeric of it all.

"Suicide represents . . . a privileged moment. . . ."
Then what keeps you—and me—from being sick of it all?

The telephones work, but I'm still cut off from you.
We star in *America,* fast epic of it all.

What shapes galaxies and keeps them from flying apart?
There's that missing mass, the black magic of it all.

What makes yours the rarest edition is just this:
it's bound in human skin, final fabric of it all.

I'm smashed, fine Enemy, in your isolate mirror.
Why the diamond display then—in public—of it all?

Before the palaver ends, hear the sparrows' songs,
the quick quick quick, O the quick of it all.

For the suicidally beautiful, autumn now starts.
Their fathers' heroes, boys gallop, kick off it all.

The sudden storm swept its ice across the great plains.
How did you find me, then, in the thick of it all?

Across the world one aches for New York, but to long
for New York in New York's most tragic of it all.

For Shahid too the night went "quickly as it came"—
After that, old friend, came the music of it all.

(FOR ANTHONY LACAVARO)

In Real Time

*Feel the patient's heart
Pounding—oh please, this once—*
——JAMES MERRILL

I'll do what I must if I'm bold in real time.
A refugee, I'll be paroled in real time.

Cool evidence clawed off like shirts of hellfire?
A former existence untold in real time . . .

The one you would choose: were you led then by him?
What longing, *O Yaar,* is controlled in real time?

Each syllable sucked under waves of our earth—
The funeral love comes to hold in real time!

They left him alive so that he could be lonely—
The god of small things is not consoled in real time.

Please afterwards empty my pockets of keys—
It's hell in the city of gold in real time.

God's angels again are—for Satan!—forlorn.
Salvation was bought but sin sold in real time.

And who is the terrorist, who the victim?
We'll know if the country is polled in real time.

"Behind a door marked DANGER" are being unwound
the prayers my friend had enscrolled in real time.

The throat of the rearview and sliding down it
the Street of Farewell's now unrolled in real time.

I heard the incessant dissolving of silk—
I felt my heart growing so old in real time.

Her heart must be ash where her body lies burned.
What hope lets your hands rake the cold in real time?

Now Friend, the Beloved has stolen your words—
Read slowly: the plot will unfold in real time.

(FOR DANIEL HALL)

Of Fire

In a mansion once of love I lit a chandelier of fire . . .
I stood on a stair of water; I stood on a stair of fire.

When, to a new ghost, I recited, "Is That What You Are,"
at the windows in the knives he combed his hair of fire.

You have remained with me even in the missing of you.
Could a financier then ask me for a new share of fire?

I keep losing this letter to the gods of abandon.
Won't you tell me how you found it—in what hemisphere of fire?

Someone stirs, after decades, in a glass mountain's ruins.
Is Death a cry from an age that was a frozen year of fire?

I have brought my life here where it must have been once,
my wings, still hope and grief, but singed by a courtier of fire.

When the Husband of Water touched his Concubine of Snow,
he hardened to melt in their private affair of fire.

Don't lose me in the crowds of this world's cities,
or the Enemy may steal from me what gods revere of fire.

The way we move into a dream we won't ever remember,
statues will now move into wars for a career of fire.

What lights up the buildings? My being turned away! O, the injustice
as I step through a hoop of tears, all I can bare of fire.

Soldier: "The enemy can see you and that's how you die."
On the world's roof, breathless, he defends a glacier of fire.

I have come down to my boat to wish myself *Bon Voyage*.
If that's the true sound of brevity, what will reappear of fire?

A designer of horizons, I've come knocking at your door.
Buy my sunsets, please, for the Pacific's interior of fire.

I could not improve my skill to get ahead of storms though
I too enrolled in Doomsday to be a courier of fire.

"on the last day of one September" "one William was born"
Native of Water, Shahid's brought the Kashmir of fire.

(FOR W. S. MERWIN)

Things

Blood, Hook & Eye: Certainly here lay true true things
for *Our Master Plan*—by the plough—among blue things.

About the death penalty—as you held back a tear—
even the children cried out that they foreknew things.

"The two houses in which I was raised were torn down."
Summers raced to autumnal lands to bedew things.

"I could not find you and feared I'd never find you . . ."
Then out of the blue you called me. You value—things?

He "can't get called / on . . . or taken to the cleaners"
though it's time for Anonymous to shampoo things.

It snowed. Then I had no home. Way way back beyond
with the exact meaning of faith I'll argue things.

Black Death inhabits his field with fascinating pain
and burns down the accrued Muslim-Christian-Jew things.

Your country also had no post office until now?
"But now no one's left to write to there"—Ah!—to do things.

I, from the upper berth, slip "down into her dream."
Choo-choo "Goes the train towards" some déjà-vu things.

I save threadbare tapestries, stained silks, ripped cashmeres.
They say, *Now's the time to buy, to be into things*.

Has a narrow bridge in a flat valley at last
led me to Paradox proper to see through things?

Silence is the keeper of the keys to secrets.
"I can't talk to my wife / but I can to you"—*THINGS!*

He goes through his motions like a ghost while I am
doomed to watch him forsake me to interview things.

Shahid, I'm *Oak,* then *Angel of rains and rivers*.
Ah well, *Dara* also, like your name, means two things.

(FOR DARA WIER)

Shines

Suspended in the garden, Time, bit by bit, shines—
As "you lean over this page, / late and alone, it shines."

I've rushed to the country in which pain is asleep.
Its capital, for your unannounced visit, shines.

O Wailing Wall O Holy Sepulchre O Far Mosque
The Tunnel echoes stones, but still no exit shines.

Reasons for moving? Sleeping with one eye open!
But *Darker's* first edition at the exhibit shines.

Dying to be cast in saffron plaster—the Brahmin's!—
a soul (they mean the Untouchable's?) in transit shines?

Water drops on the burner its sizzling red pearls.
Moonlight, nude on the apricots of Gilgit, shines.

"The mirror / is in the living room. / You are there."
The cold place one body took—which I'll inhabit—shines.

WHAT THE THUNDER SAID Shantih Shantih Shantih
The peace that passeth understanding in Sanskrit shines.

Have you invented an ending that comes out right?
Judgment Day is already here, and no Writ shines.

Mark how Shahid returns your very words to you—
It's when the heart, still unbriefed, but briefly lit, shines.

(FOR MARK STRAND)

My Word

I am lying even now—I give you my word.
Kind of a picnic, an occupied shoe. My word!

My telegram arrives, no one's there to read it—
not even he who on tombs will bedew my word.

Danger invites rescue, we have a good thing going.
So let's break everything, please rescue my word.

The ghost said nothing that added to our knowledge.
Upon the candle—which lit itself—who blew my word?

I'm at home, betrothed to blue, with her refracted light.
The light is home, this blue is blue all through my word.

Hard to say who's winning. Nobody is winning.
Kansas City! Oriental art! Big Zoo! My word!

I took the shortest route through Belief's sad country
when archangels, on the Word's command, slew my word.

This erasure tilts words toward memory or tilts
against your word—at the tiny hour of two—my word.

Forgive me, please, could we be alone forever?
I have never been alone; I'll live to rue my word.

Our silence, Beloved Enemy, is not beyond
whatever love has done to your word, to my word.

Now don't put on, please, that face, just wait for me here.
I stand no one up. See you in a few. My word.

Will the barbarians bring again their invisible language?
They were the solution, they foreknew my word.

Yours too, Shahid, will be a radical departure.
You'll go out of yourself and then into my word.

(FOR JAMES TATE)

From The Start

The Beloved will leave you behind from the start.
Light is difficult: one must be blind from the start.

You begin to feel better when the clocks are set back?
Child of northern darkness—so defined from the start.

Between two snow-heavy boughs, perhaps a bright star?
Or in one sparkling many stars combined from the start?

Ontological episode? God doesn't care.
"That is why he exists," you divined from the start.

Solomon's throne was a toy, his Judgment mere talk—
Only our sins must be enshrined from the start.

Poet, tell me again how the white heron rises.
For the spirit, they say, is confined from the start.

To *What is mind?* we swiftly answer *O, no matter!*
Those who know matter never mind from the start.

Will the middle class give up its white devotions?
Feed their infants cayenne and tamarind from the start.

I am mere dust. The desert hides itself in me.
Against me the ocean has reclined from the start.

Who but Satan can know God's sorrow in Heaven?
God longs for the lover He undermined from the start.

"But I / am here in this real life / that I was given. . . ."
To what else should we be resigned from the start?

You have dwelt at the root of a scream forever—
The Forever Shahid's countersigned from the start.

(FOR HAYDEN CARRUTH)

Angels

The pure pain with which he recognizes angels
has left him without cures among the dreamless angels.

The dawn looked over its shoulder to ask the naked night
for the new fashions in which it could dress angels.

Is it that I've been searching in the wrong places for you?
That your address is still Los Angeles, Angels?

The air is my vinegar, I, its perfect preserve—
Watch how I'm envied by Heaven's meticulous angels.

In Inferno the walls mirror brocades and silks.
Satan's legions—though fallen—are, nonetheless, angels.

"Let there be Light," He said. "And the music of the spheres."
To what tune does one set *The Satanic Verses,* Angels?

I won't lift, off the air, any wingprints, O God—
Hire raw detectives to track down the mutinous angels.

All day we call it wisdom but then again at night
it's only pain as it comes from the darkness, Angels!

Why is God so frightened of my crazy devotion to Him?
Does he think that, like Satan, I too will finesse angels?

Do they dye their wings after Forever, tinting their haloes,
aging zero without Time, those androgynous angels?

You play innocence so well, with such precision, Shahid:
You could seduce God Himself, and fuck the sexless angels.

Of Water

But first the screened mirror, all I knew of water!
Imagine "the thirstquenching virtue of water."

Who "kept on building castles" "Upon a certain rock"
"Glacial warden over 'dreams come true' " of water?

Of course, I saw Chile in my rearview mirror,
it's disappeared under a curfew of water.

Hagar, in shards, reflects her shattered Ishmael.
Call her the desert Muslim—or Jew—of water.*

God, Wordless, beheld the pulled rain but missed the held sun . . .
The Rainbow—that Arrow!—Satan's coup of water.

Don't beckon me, Love, to the island of your words—
You yourself reached it, erasing my view of water.

Her star-cold palanquin goes with the caravan.
Majnoon, now she'll be news—out of the blue—of water.

When the Beast takes off his mask, Love, let it be you
sweetening Tomorrow Doom's taboo of water.

No need to stop the ears to the Sirens' rhetoric;
just mock their rock-theme, you skeleton crew of water.

Are your streets, Abraham, washed of "the Sons of Stones"?
Sand was all Ishmael once drew of water.

I have signed, O my enemy, your death-warrant.
I won't know in time I am like you of water.

For God's sake don't unveil the Black Stone of K'aaba.
What if Faith too's let love bead a dew of water?

I have even become tears to live in your eyes.
If you weep, Stark Lover, for my breakthrough of water?

Shahid's junk mail has surfaced in a dead-letter office.
He's deluxed in the leather *Who's Who of Water*.

* When Hagar and Ishmael were left in the desert, God answered Hagar's plea for
 water for the infant Ishmael with the Zumzum spring in Mecca.

As Ever

(after Ahmad Faraz)

So I'll regret it. But lead my heart to pain.
Return, if it is just to leave me again.

"Till death do us part." Come for their sense of *us* . . .
For Belief's sake, let appearances remain.

Let YOU, at Elysian Fields, step off the streetcar—
so my sense of wonder's made utterly plain.

Not for mine but for the world's sake come back.
They ask why you left? To whom all must I explain?

I laughed when they said our time was running out—
I stirred the leaves in the tea I'd brewed to drain.

Break your pride, be the Consoler for once—
Bring roses, let my love-illusion remain.

An era's passed since the luxury of tears—
Make me weep, Consoler, let blood know its rain.

From New York to Andalusia I searched for you—
Lorca, dazzled on your lips, is all of Spain.

"Time, like Love, wears a mask in this story."
And Love? My blind spot. Piercing me to the brain.

Oh, that my head were waters, mine eyes a fountain
so that I might weep day and night for the slain.

Shouting your name till the last car had disappeared,
how I ran on the platform after your train.

To find her, 'round phantom-wrists I glue bangles—
What worlds she did not break when she left my lane!

Still beguiled with hopes of you, the heart is lit.
To put out this last candle, come, it burns in vain.

Land

Swear by the olive in the God-kissed land—
There is no sugar in the promised land.

Why must the bars turn neon now when, Love,
I'm already drunk in your capitalist land?

If home is found on both sides of the globe,
home is of course here—and always a missed land.

The hour's come to redeem the pledge (not wholly?)
in Fate's "Long years ago we made a tryst" land.

Clearly, these men were here only to destroy,
a mosque now the dust of a prejudiced land.

Will the Doomsayers die, bitten with envy,
when springtime returns to our dismissed land?

The prisons fill with the cries of children.
Then how do you subsist, how do you persist, Land?

"Is my love nothing for I've borne no children?"
I'm with you, Sappho, in that anarchist land.

A hurricane is born when the wings flutter . . .
Where will the butterfly, on my wrist, land?

You made me wait for one who wasn't even there
though summer had finished in that tourist land.

Do the blind hold temples close to their eyes
when we steal their gods for our atheist land?

Abandoned bride, Night throws down her jewels
so Rome—on our descent—is an amethyst land.

At the moment the heart turns terrorist,
are Shahid's arms broken, O Promised Land?

(FOR CHRISTOPHER MERRILL)

Not All, Only A Few Return

(after Ghalib)

Just a few return from dust, disguised as roses.
What hopes the earth forever covers, what faces?

I too could recall moonlit roofs, those nights of wine—
But Time has shelved them now in Memory's dimmed places.

She has left forever, let blood flow from my eyes
till my eyes are lamps lit for love's darkest places.

All is his—Sleep, Peace, Night—when on his arm your hair
shines to make him the god whom nothing effaces.

With wine, the palm's lines, believe me, rush to Life's stream—
Look, here's my hand, and here the red glass it raises.

See me! Beaten by sorrow, man is numbed to pain.
Grief has become the pain only pain erases.

World, should Ghalib keep weeping you will see a flood
drown your terraced cities, your marble palaces.

Even The Rain

What will suffice for a true-love knot? Even the rain?
But he has bought grief's lottery, bought even the rain.

"Our glosses / wanting in this world"—Can you remember?
Anyone!—"when we thought / the poets taught" even the rain?

After we died—*That was it!*—God left us in the dark.
And as we forgot the dark, we forgot even the rain.

Drought was over. Where was I? Drinks were on the house.
For mixers, my love, you'd poured—what?—even the rain.

Of this pear-shaped orange's perfumed twist, I will say:
Extract Vermouth from the bergamot, even the rain.

How did the Enemy love you—with earth? air? and fire?
He held just one thing back till he got even: the rain.

This is God's site for a new house of executions?
You swear by the Bible, Despot, even the rain?

After the bones—those flowers—this was found in the urn:
The lost river, ashes from the ghat, even the rain.

What was I to prophesy if not the end of the world?
A salt pillar for the lonely lot, even the rain.

How the air raged, desperate, streaming the earth with flames—
To help burn down my house, Fire sought even the rain.

He would raze the mountains, he would level the waves;
he would, to smooth his epic plot, even the rain.

New York belongs at daybreak to only me, just me—
To make this claim Memory's brought even the rain.

They've found the knife that killed you, but whose prints are these?
No one has such small hands, Shahid, not even the rain.

Water

When pilgrims brought back no bottles of Samarkand water,
everyone filled our samovars with almond water.

There was only a tea of the second water
we remembered home samovars with cinnamoned water.

As soon as springtime came in every house
we drank tea steeped in cardamom and almond water.

The floods left little of our land to us
but how grateful we were for the unsunned water.

A terrible time is coming *après vous après vous*
What fire will you find to refund water?

At the temple and the mosque the rose petals
lay all night perfuming the stunned water.

This may surprise you but after the forty days
the sunshine left us helpless with stunned water.

It was a dark time and everywhere the soldiers
had made sure we were thirsty for their garrisoned water.

So if this is indeed a matter of nature then the sky
was the flesh and its reflection was skeletoned water.

What did your ancestor bring from Samarkand? Water?
In our samovars it becomes cardamom and almond water.

Of Snow

Husband of Water, where is your Concubine of Snow?
Has she laced your flooded desert with a wine of snow?

What a desert we met in—the foliage was lush!—
a cactus was dipped into every moonshine of snow.

One song is so solitaire in our ring of mountains,
its echo climbs to cut itself at each line of snow.

The sky beyond its means is always besides itself
till (by the plane) each peak rises, a shrine of snow.

Snowmen, inexplicably, have gathered in the Sahara
to melt and melt and melt for a Palestine of snow.

Kali turned to ice one winter, her veins transparent—
On her lips blood froze. A ruby wine of snow!

If Lorca were alive he would again come to New York,
bringing back to my life that one Valentine of snow.

Do you need to make angels, really, who then vanish
or are angels all you can undermine of snow?

I who believe in prayer but could never in God
place roses at your grave with nothing to divine of snow.

When he drinks in winter, Shahid kisses his enemies.
For Peace, then, let bars open at the first sign of snow.

Air

Drink this rain-dark rum of air
column of breath column of air.

About Me

(after some lines of Wisława Szymborska)

I'm too close, too close for him to dream about me,
for he is held (he is *al-Mustalim*) about me.

Now the grace to disappear from astonished eyes!
Note how I possess this—love's last!—theme about me.

Not so, my lord. "Seems," madam? Nay, it is. O God!
I am too much in the sun. I know not "seems" about me.

On the head of each pin dance the fallen angels.
If only they would needle the Supreme about me!

I pull my arm out from under his sleeping head,
limited to my own form, my scream about me.

My ears catch the rustling of last wills torn to pieces—
The dead so poor, infatuated, teem about me.

Now Christ will never die so readily for you,
left nailed with His wounds' sorry regime about me.

A house is on fire without my calling for help.
Like fangs in the dark, windowpanes gleam about me.

Elusively gay but not quite presently straight,
one is stone in his own forest stream about me.

On Doomsday God asked the Pure, "Why didn't you sin?
Didn't you trust the best (*ar-Rahim*) about Me?"

I read letters of the dead and am a helpless god,
their bad taste, their electrical steam about me.

Father of Clay, this is Shahid; I am become flesh—
No spirit dusts or will itself redeem about me.

Note: *al-Mustalim* ("the enraptured" in Arabic).

      ar-Rahim ("The Merciful"—one of God's ninety-nine names in Arabic. The traditional Muslim prayer begins: "Begin in the Name of God, the Beneficent, the Merciful").

In Marble

Because there's no thyme or fenugreek in marble,
they say, "Let's go and play hide-and-seek in marble."

There on the tower (our life, our life, our life)—
watch the gull open and shut its beak in marble.

On her temple's black walls, Kali prints her tiger's
gold-red stripes till all's as if batik in marble.

Go where I will? Where will I go? Who hears my song
now that justice is radical chic in marble.

My lover went to Chisti's mother-of-pearl tomb
and almost found, calligraphed, my shriek in marble.

To be reduced to God's tears, from Heaven to Hell,
angels wail, and that too cheek-to-cheek in marble.

A penniless voyeur, I go downtown to see
Rodin's lovers—in one gift shop—peak in marble.

A hand broke. It was in plaster. I took it in mine.
He who was a god is now so bleak in marble.

Of course, I'll say something about the Taj Mahal
silvering in the moonlight all week in marble.

The sky, beyond itself, was besides itself when
above the clouds it saw mountains peak in marble.

From whose lips will a remembered god breathe at last?
If I am left mute, let someone else speak in marble.

Farewell, you museum-people, now leave me to face
my oracle spoken by an antique in marble.

Apollo (for weary way-worn wandering Shahid)
is yet another heartbreaking Greek in marble.

Bones

(after Hart Crane)

"I, too, was liege / To rainbows currying" pulsant bones.
The "sun took step of" Brooklyn Bridge's resonant bones.

From Far Rockaway to Golden Gate I saw blood
washed up on streets against God's irrelevant bones.

If the soul were a body, what would it insist on?
On smooth skin? On stubborn flesh? Or on elegant bones?

"The window goes blond slowly." And I beside you
am stripped and stripped and stripped to luxuriant bones.

So Elizabeth had two hundred Catholics burned
(Bloody Mary had loved the smoke of Protestant bones).

In the hair of Pocahontas a forest shudders.
Inventions cobblestone her extravagant bones.

They refuse to burn when we set fire to the flesh—
those flowers float down the Ganges as adamant bones.

"Footprints on the Glacier" are the snowman's—or mine?
Whoever, they're found under some hesitant bones.

Someone once told us he had lost his pity for
(he did not qualify with "ignorant" or "tolerant") bones.

Migrating from me to me to me the soul asks
a bit seriously: what is our covenant, Bones?

Mustard oil, when heated, breaks out in veins which then
cayenne the sacrificed goat's most compliant bones.

The troops left our haven hanging in the night and said
the child's skeleton was made of militant bones.

And so it was Shahid entered the broken world
when everyone had bypassed the heart's expectant bones.

In

God to aggrandise, God to glorify
—GERARD MANLEY HOPKINS

Now "God to aggrandise, God to glorify" in
the candle that "clear burns"—glare I can't come by in.

What else for night-travel? The extra pair of socks?
Besides the tin of tea, pack the anti-fly in.

If you don't succeed at first, do certainly give up—
I too shut off those who say *Just keep tryin'!*

Galloping flood, hooves iron by the river's edge—
Heart, this beating night, how will you rein the sky in?

Thank you for the parchment and the voice of the sea.
A drowned god used the shell to send his reply in.

When the last leaves were birds, stuck wingless to branches,
the wind glass-stormed the season you'd left me to cry in.

Flood the market, O Blood, so the liver is restored,
again emotion's sea, the heart's forsaken tie-in.

By the Enemy, after battle, I place flowers
and the swords he'd heard the angels' lullaby in.

When even God is dead, what is left but prayer?
And this wilderness, the mirrors I multiply in?

When you missed its "feet and fur," JM, I too mourned
the caterpillar spring had sent the butterfly in.

Doomsday is over, Eden stretched vast before me—
I see the rooms, all the rooms, I am to die in.

Ere he never returns, he whose footsteps are dying,
Shahid, run out weeping, bring that passerby in.

Beyond English

No language is old—or young—beyond English.
So what of a common tongue beyond English?

I know some words for war, all of them sharp,
but the sharpest one is *jung*—beyond English!

If you wish to know of a king who loved his slave,
you must learn legends, often-sung, beyond English.

Baghdad is sacked and its citizens must watch
prisoners (now in miniatures) hung beyond English.

Go all the way through *jungle* from *aleph* to *zenith*
to see English, like monkeys, swung beyond English.

So never send to know for whom the bell tolled,
for across the earth it has rung beyond English.

If you want your drugs legal you must leave the States,
not just for hashish but one—*bhung*—beyond English.

Heartbroken, I tottered out "into windless snow,"
snowflakes on my lips, silence stung beyond English.

When the phrase, "The Mother of all Battles," caught on,
the surprise was indeed not sprung beyond English.

Could a soul crawl away at last unshriveled which
to its "own fusing senses" had clung beyond English?

If someone asks where Shahid has disappeared,
he's waging a war (no, *jung*) beyond English.

(FOR LAWRENCE NEEDHAM)

Of Light

At dawn you leave. The river wears its skin of light.
And I trace love's loss to the origin of light.

"I swallow down the goodbyes I won't get to use."
At grief's speed she waves from a palanquin of light.

My book's been burned? Send me the ashes, so I can say:
I've been sent the phoenix in a coffin of light.

From History tears learn a slanted understanding
of the human face torn by blood's bulletin of light.

It was a temporal thought. Well, it has vanished.
Will Prometheus commit the mortal sin of light?

She said, "My name is icicles coming down from it . . ."
Did I leave it, somewhere, in a margin of light?

When I go off alone, as if listening for God,
there's absolutely nothing I can win of light.

Now everything's left to the imagination—
a djinn has deprived even Aladdin of light.

We'll see Manhattan, a bride in diamonds, one day
abashed to remind her sweet man, Brooklyn, of light.

"A cheekbone, / A curved piece of brow, / A pale eyelid . . ."
And the dark eye I make out with all within of light.

Stranger, when the river leans toward the emptiness,
abandon, for my darkness, the thick and thin of light.

"On these beaches / the sea throws itself down, in flames"
as we bring back, at sunset, the incarnadine of light.

Again on the point of giving away my heart,
Life is stalked by Fog, that blond assassin of light.

One day the streets all over the world will be empty;
from every tomb I'll learn all we imagine of light.

Galway, somehow with you in Freedom, New Hampshire,
Shahid won't let Death make of Love a ruin of light.

(FOR GALWAY KINNELL)

Stars

When through night's veil they continue to seep, stars
in infant galaxies begin to weep stars.

After the eclipse, there were no cheap stars
How can you be so cheap, stars?

How grateful I am you stay awake with me
till by dawn, like you, I'm ready to sleep, stars!

If God sows sunset embers in you, Shahid,
all night, because of you, the world will reap stars.

For Time

You who searched the world for a brave rhyme for time
got real lucky with a Guggenheim for time.

At the shrine I'll offer not roses but clocks.
When I return, I will have no time for time.

After the first death, there's only the first, which
with each death is now your paradigm for time.

All summer the news from the lost peaks said that
soldiers had died simply in a climb for time.

From new springtimes gather your loot of blossoms.
Let Kashmir arrest you for a crime for time.

Must we always cook with heartless substitutes?
Caraway for cumin *and* cloves? And lime for thyme?

When the blade became secretary to steel,
the knife's sanctuary was made sublime for time.

You never belonged even to yourself though
as you abandoned me your cry was *I'm for time*.

What a wonderful party! It is the Sabbath!
And everyone's cry is "Le Chaim." For time?

I really need a drink to be able to drink!
That clink—cracking ice—crystals my chime for time.

The Country of the Blind has ordered mirrors.
Its one-eyed king's vision is now prime for time.

The gravestones are filled with poetry or pathos?
Well, you knew the war was a pantomime for time.

Who amputates clock-hands to make you, Shahid,
await the god not there with all the time for time?

God

Of all things He's the King Allah King God.
Then why this fear of idolizing God?

Outgunned Chechens hold off Russian tanks—
They have a prayer. Are you listening, God?

I begged for prayers to the Surgeon's answer,
my heart alone against terrorizing God.

Masked, I hold him enthralled who's harmed me most—
I will hurt him as he's been hurting God.

So what make you of cosmic background noise?
Well, there's the Yoni (*My!*) and the Ling (*God!*).

A butterfly's wings flutter in the rain.
In which storm looms the fabricating God?

I believe in prayer and the need to believe—
even the great Nothing signifying God.

Of Fidelity I've made such high style
that, jealous of my perfect devotion,
even the angels come down from Heaven
and beg—beg—me to stop worshipping God.

How come you simply do not age, Shahid?
Well, I wish everyone well, including God.

Forever

Even Death won't hide the poor fugitive forever;
on Doomsday he will learn he must live forever.

Is that nectar the cry of the desert prophets?
See angels pour the Word through a sieve forever.

On the gibbet Hallaj cried *I Am the Truth*.
In this universe one dies a plaintive forever.

When parents fall in love with those blond assassins,
their children sign up for Western Civ forever.

With a brief note he quit the Dead Letter Office—
O World, they've lost Bartleby's missive forever.

Am I some Sinai, Moses, for lightning to char?
See me solarized, in negative forever.

In the heart's wild space lies the space of wilderness.
What won't one lose, what home one won't give forever!

A perfect stranger, he greeted herself in joy—
Not to be Tom, how lovely—she said—*I'm Viv forever!*

Jamshed, inventor of wine, saw the world in his cup.
Drink, cried his courtiers, *for he won't live forever.*

He lives by his wits, wears blue all day, stars all night.
Who would have guessed God would be a spiv forever?

Will the Enemy smile as I pass him on the street?
I'm still searching for someone to forgive forever.

As landscapes rise like smoke from their eyes, the blind hear
God swear by the fig and the olive forever.

The Hangman washes his hands, puts his son to sleep.
But for whom, come dawn, he's decisive forever?

Alone in His Cave—His Dance done—He's smeared with ash.
The Ganges flows from the head of Shiv forever.

You've forgiven everyone, Shahid, even God—
Then how could someone like you not live forever?

(FOR DONALD REVELL)

After You

We are left mute and so much is left unnamed after you—
No one is left in this world to be blamed after you.

Someone has disappeared after christening Bertha—
Shahid, will a hurricane ever be named after you?

Now from Miami to Boston Bertha is breaking her bones—
I find her in the parking lot. She says, "I'm blamed after you."

The Deluge would happen—it was claimed—after you
But the world did go on, unashamed, after you

ANDREW BERTHA CHARLES DAVID ELLA FLOYD GEORGE
    but S comes so late in the alphabet that although
SHAHID DEVASTATES FLORIDA is your dream headline,
    no hurricane will ever be named after you.

In Arabic

(with revisions of some couplets of "Arabic")

A language of loss? I have some business in Arabic.
Love letters: calligraphy pitiless in Arabic.

At an exhibit of miniatures, what Kashmiri hairs!
Each paisley inked into a golden tress in Arabic.

This much fuss about a language I don't know? So one day
perfume from a dress may let you digress in Arabic.

A "Guide for the Perplexed" was written—believe me—
by Cordoba's Jew—Maimonides—in Arabic.

Majnoon, by stopped caravans, rips his collars, cries "Laila!"
Pain translated is O! much more—not less—in Arabic.

Writes Shammas: Memory, no longer confused, now is a homeland—
his two languages a Hebrew caress in Arabic.

When Lorca died, they left the balconies open and saw:
On the sea his *qasidas* stitched seamless in Arabic.

In the Veiled One's harem, an adulteress hanged by eunuchs—
So the rank mirrors revealed to Borges in Arabic.

Ah, bisexual Heaven: wide-eyed houris and immortal youths!
To your each desire they say *Yes! O Yes!* in Arabic.

For that excess of sibilance, the last Apocalypse,
so pressing those three forms of S in Arabic.

I too, O Amichai, saw everything, just like you did—
In Death. In Hebrew. And (please let me stress) in Arabic.

They ask me to tell them what *Shahid* means: Listen, listen:
It means "The Beloved" in Persian, "witness" in Arabic.

Tonight

Pale hands I loved beside the Shalimar

Where are you now? Who lies beneath your spell tonight?
Whom else from rapture's road will you expel tonight?

Those "Fabrics of Cashmere—" "to make Me beautiful—"
"Trinket"—to gem—"Me to adorn—How tell"—tonight?

I beg for haven: Prisons, let open your gates—
A refugee from Belief seeks a cell tonight.

God's vintage loneliness has turned to vinegar—
All the archangels—their wings frozen—fell tonight.

Lord, cried out the idols, *Don't let us be broken;*
Only we can convert the infidel tonight.

Mughal ceilings, let your mirrored convexities
multiply me at once under your spell tonight.

He's freed some fire from ice in pity for Heaven.
He's left open—for God—the doors of Hell tonight.

In the heart's veined temple, all statues have been smashed.
No priest in saffron's left to toll its knell tonight.

God, limit these punishments, there's still Judgment Day—
I'm a mere sinner, I'm no infidel tonight.

Executioners near the woman at the window.
Damn you, Elijah, I'll bless Jezebel tonight.

The hunt is over, and I hear the Call to Prayer
fade into that of the wounded gazelle tonight.

My rivals for your love—you've invited them all?
This is mere insult, this is no farewell tonight.

And I, Shahid, only am escaped to tell thee—
God sobs in my arms. Call me Ishmael tonight.

Existed

If you leave who will prove that my cry existed?
Tell me what was I like before I existed.

About the Author

Agha Shahid Ali, a Kashmiri-American, was born on February 4, 1949, in New Delhi and grew up in Kashmir. He was educated at the University of Kashmir, Srinagar, and the University of Delhi. Shahid came to America in his early twenties and earned his Ph.D. at Pennsylvania State University in 1984 and his M.F.A in Poetry at the University of Arizona in 1985. He taught at Hamilton College in New York, then became director of the M.F.A. Creative Writing program at the University of Massachusetts in Amherst. He also taught at the University of Utah and in the M.F.A. Program for Writers at Warren Wilson College. In the spring of 2000, Shahid was a visiting poet in the Graduate Creative Writing Program at N.Y.U. Agha Shahid Ali's volumes of poetry include *Bone-Sculpture* (1972), *In Memory of Begum Akhtar & Other Poems* (1979), *The Half-Inch Himalayas* (1987), *A Walk Through the Yellow Pages* (1987), *A Nostalgist's Map of America* (1991), *The Beloved Witness: Selected Poems* (1992), *The Country Without a Post Office* (1997), and *Rooms Are Never Finished* (2001). Shahid also translated Faiz Ahmed Faiz's collection *The Rebel's Silhouette: Selected Poems* and was the editor of *Ravishing DisUnities: Real Ghazals in English*. He was awarded Guggenheim and Ingram-Merrill fellowships and a Pushcart Prize, and his collection *Rooms Are Never Finished* was a finalist for the National Book Award in 2001. Agha Shahid Ali died on December 8, 2001.